Croydon
Between the Wars

Photographs from the period 1919 to 1939

Frontispiece – Map of central and south Croydon – Scale 6″ to 1 mile
This is reproduced from the 1932 edition of the Ordnance Survey. Railway sidings and workshops still covered the Fairfield site. (See illustration number 91, pages 40 and 41).

Most of the Waddon estate had been completed and the new Whitgift School was open at Haling Park, just below the centre of the page. Most of the streets and built-up area shown here had in fact already been developed by 1900, or soon after.

Front Cover
This view of High Street about 1936 is from the corner of Surrey Street, with the sign of the Bodega restaurant on the extreme right. This was the 17th century Ship inn which became the Bodega around 1914, its name reverting to the Ship again in the mid 1950s. Next door but one is the National Provincial bank (now National Westminster) on the corner of Katharine Street, with the Croydon public house on the other corner. Beyond are Staple's art shop, the historic Hammond and Hussey's ironmongers and the town's principal and oldest inn, the 15th century Greyhound Hotel. These buildings were replaced by the St. George's Walk development in the 1960s.

Back Cover
This view of Croydon Airport dates from about 1932. One of the Imperial Airways new Handley Page HP 42s G AAUD – 'Hanno' is flying over the new airport buildings. Purley Way is in the foreground. For years the fastest airliner for its payload, with a cruising speed of 100 mph, it is often claimed that the HP 42 was the most comfortable aircraft ever. Eight were built and they were a familiar sight at Croydon until the outbreak of war in 1939.

Croydon Airport was the scene of many remarkable firsts in civil aviation and had the world's first purpose built airport hotel and terminal buildings. The name of Croydon became known all over the world and even today many people know of the town only because of its famous airport. It finally closed in 1959.

Contents

Editor John B. Gent, M.C.I.T.

Published by the Croydon Natural History and Scientific Society Limited

96a Brighton Road
South Croydon
Surrey CR2 6AD

ISBN: 0 906047 07 2

Printed by Design & Print (Sussex) Ltd
Portslade, Brighton, East Sussex

48 pages   104 illustrations

First edition—November 1987
Second edition—November 1992

Price £4.75

The Disappearing Countryside

This publication is the third in a series intended as a visual record of Croydon during different periods. *Victorian Croydon Illustrated* covers the period from the 1830s to 1901. *Edwardian Croydon Illustrated* covers 1901 until the end of the First World War and this deals with 1919 to 1939.

A publication such as this can however give only a very general impression of a period. It is certainly not a history but it can highlight a few interesting features of the time. Most of the scenes in the following pages will bring back memories to older people. They show Croydon appearing very different from today though in many instances it has changed little physically. There was already plenty of traffic but the suburban roads looked much tidier without the parked cars of today. The horse was still quite commonly used, especially by tradesmen such as milkmen, bakers, greengrocers, and coal merchants for their regular deliveries to the door. Class distinctions were still carefully observed: many houses had separate entrances for tradespeople. Nearly everyone wore a hat.

Poverty, worsened by the depression, was common particularly in areas such as Forster and Wilford Roads, known as 'bang 'ole' or 'bang all' possibly because any stranger venturing there might expect an unfriendly reception. Wounded ex-servicemen could frequently be seen selling matches or bootlaces on street corners. This was in contrast with the Sunday 'Monkey Parade' in the town centre when many Croydonians donned their best attire and walked around the streets, seeing and being seen.

After the horrors of the First World War there was a tremendous surge in the idea of freedom. There was a strong feeling that women should have some say in the formation of government and they were actually allowed to vote on reaching the age of 30. There was more freedom too in dress although most schools insisted on uniforms.

So far as wages and prices are concerned, comparison is always rather difficult because generalisations are not very meaningful and living standards and expectations change with progress. Prices had risen sharply in 1914 and continued to do so until 1920 when they were some 2½ times higher. In most cases wages had by then just about caught up. Following a brief economic boom at the end of the war, there was a period of rapidly falling prices from 1920, and this was accompanied by reductions in wages. For ten years after 1923 prices fell at a much more moderate rate but wages were reasonably stable. However many people were unemployed and for them it was a difficult time with barely enough for survival. Prices then moved slowly upwards until the outbreak of war in 1939 when the cost of living was some two thirds higher than in 1914 but lower than in 1920.

A comparison of some typical average annual wages and salaries shows the following;

	1922/24	1935/37
	£	£
Doctor	756	1094
Bank Clerk	280	368
Foreman	268	273
Railway engine driver	276	258
Shop assistant	120	173
Agricultural labourer	82	89

As examples of prices, in 1919 detached double-fronted houses with four bedrooms were available for £950, a smaller house for £700, and an unfurnished flat with two rooms could be rented at £8 monthly. A good quality oak gate-legged table cost £3 17s 6d to £5 7s 6d depending on size. A 1lb tin of coffee cost 2s 10d, pale ale 5s 4d a crate (12 bottles) and gin 10s 0d a bottle.

In 1939 new three-bedroomed houses were advertised at prices between £595 and £925 and could be rented for 23s 0d weekly, whilst a furnished flat of four rooms could be rented for 35s 0d weekly. A day trip by train and boat to Dieppe cost 17s 9d, and a 12 day coach tour to Scotland was advertised at £16 16s 0d. Women's Harris tweed suits and coats could each be obtained for £2 2s 0d and 'absolutely painless' dental extractions were 1s 0d. Zeeta's restaurant in George Street offered special summer luncheons at 1s 9d.

The following conversion table should be used where references to pre-decimal currency occur.

Pre-Decimal	Decimal
1d (penny)	just under ½p
6d	2½p
1s 0d (shilling)	5p
2s 6d	12½p

Croydon was a county borough and in 1921 the population was 190,877. The parish of Addington was included in the borough from 1928 and at the 1931 cenus the population had risen to 233,115 whilst in 1939 it was estimated at 243,400.

The Coulsdon and Purley urban district included Selsdon, Sanderstead, Kenley, Coulsdon and Purley, with a population in 1921 of 21,491, in 1931 37,702 and in 1939 estimated at 61,710. These areas became part of the newly formed London Borough of Croydon in 1965. Although not in Croydon between the wars they have been included in this publication.

In 1919 Croydon still had quite a lot of open country within its borders. Shirley, Addington and Waddon were predominantly rural as were some parts of Addiscombe, South and Upper Norwood, and Norbury. There were a number of large houses with their own small estates and most of the larger Victorian and Edwardian houses were still in family occupation, often with resident maids and other domestic helpers. Market gardens flourished in Bensham Lane and other parts of Thornton Heath and the cattle market in Selsdon Road was held weekly until 1935. Brickfields at Green Lane, Whitehorse Lane and Woodside contributed their products towards the new houses.

In the county borough there were in 1919 some 180 miles of road and 15½ miles of footpath. These figures had increased to 253 and 17 respectively by 1939.

In Coulsdon and Purley, the downland settlements of Selsdon, Sanderstead and Coulsdon were almost totally rural in 1919. Most of the built up areas were in the valleys and on the lower ground near the railways. During the war, motor vehicles had become increasingly reliable and cars soon became more common. The London General Omnibus Company and Thomas Tilling already ran a number of bus services in the district, often in competition with the trams. These bus routes were soon extended further afield and in 1921 the East Surrey Traction Company commenced running into Croydon from the country areas and towns to the south. These improvements made for easier access to places away from the railways and tram routes and this encouraged housing development.

1 Marlpit Lane – 1st May 1929

This view shows the transformation of Marlpit Lane from a narrow, rutted lane with tall hedges into the modern thoroughfare of today. Until the late 1920s Marlpit Farm was the only building in the lane above Downs Road and it survives as number 22. The houses in Downs Road can be seen clearly and behind them is the splendid avenue of trees at Cane Hill. In the background, building work is about to commence in Julien Road and Bramley Avenue as part of the development of Smitham Downs. At the bottom of Marlpit Lane are the new houses in Chaldon Way.

This photograph, taken from below Stoneyfield Road, with the first house on the left being number 60, illustrates the intense building activity which changed Coulsdon from a rural area of open downland and scattered farms. The development became possible on the death of Edmund Byron, Lord of the Manor for 58 years, and last squire of Coulsdon, who died in 1921. Coulsdon and Purley Urban District Council then purchased the title and on both sides of Brighton Road large areas of downland were built upon and enormous changes came to a village hitherto peaceful, rural and little changing.

Much of the remaining open country was soon covered with houses, many in the mock tudor style then so popular. Schools, churches, shopping parades and factories occupied other vacant plots. There were other improvements in transport as electric trains gradually replaced steam, and pneumatic tyres and covered tops were introduced on buses. By the 1930s increasing road traffic and competition from more modern buses caused the tram to fall from favour and after all local road public transport came under the control of the new London Passenger Transport Board in 1933, trolleybuses began to replace the trams.

Municipal and local enterprise probably reached its peak in 1930 with Croydon as a county borough having its own water and electricity undertakings, tramways, fire brigade, ambulance service, hospitals and courts in addition to all the other responsibilities it retains today. In 1919 there were only some 360 acres of parks and open space. By 1939 this had increased to nearly 1170 acres although not all was open to the public.

For those who could afford it plenty of choice existed for leisure activities. Sport, particularly football, tennis, golf and bowls flourished. The parks, with their brass band concerts, attracted crowds as did the boating lake in Wandle Park. The surrounding countryside was increasingly popular with hikers and cyclists. Dances were enthusiastically supported and although eating out was nothing like so common as it is today, there were a number of local venues such as the Greyhound, the King's Arms and the Café Royal in North End which was run by the Pazzi family for some 60 years until the 1950s. Tea shops abounded and Zeeta's, the Merry Kettle and Wilson's were very popular. Organisations including the Croydon Philharmonic Society, Croydon Symphony Orchestra, Croydon Stagers, Croydon Light Opera Club, Croydon Players, and Croydon Histrionic Society gave regular performances at local theatres and halls such as the Public Halls in George Street, or the North End Brotherhood Hall (later the Civic Hall). These and the Baths Hall in Scarbrook Road (the 'Winter Gardens') and the Stanley Halls amongst others also provided the setting for lectures, concerts, flower shows and many other activities.

The somewhat faded glories of the Crystal Palace and its grounds still attracted many people and the firework displays lit the sky on Thursday evenings, until the greatest display of all in 1936 when the building was sadly destroyed by fire. Professional live theatre was at various times provided at the Greyhound, the Croydon Repertory in Wellesley Road, the Grand and the Empire. The gramophone and the wireless were growing home attractions and in the mid 1930s television first made its appearance, but probably the greatest attraction of the period was the cinema.

By the beginning of the 1920s the borough had no less than eleven cinemas. In North End was the Croydon Picture House, later to become the Odeon and only recently closed. At 64, now part of Woolworths, was the Palladium which had started life in 1911 as the Cinematograph Theatre. Next to, and later incorporated in Allders was the Scala, and on the other side of the road opposite the Picture House the Princes, opened in 1921. In the same year South Norwood's Central Hall received a rival in the New Gaiety which must have seemed quite superior with its orchestra and a pipe organ which came from the home of Sir August Manns, former musical director at the Crystal Palace.

By the mid 1920s cinemas were becoming larger and more palatial. The Davis family, who had a small circuit of cinemas in London, sold them and built a super cinema in Croydon High Street which opened in 1928 (for details see illustration 11 page 8). The arrival of talkies in 1928 gave the cinema a boom for the next twenty years. A.C. Matthews (with the ten gallon hat) built two cinemas at Upper Norwood and one at Thornton Heath between 1929 and 1932. At Purley the Regal and the Astoria were rivals. The latter advertised a café and a magnificent Compton organ played by the young Robin Richmond. In 1936 and 1937 ABC opened the Savoy in London Road and the Rex in Norbury opposite the original Norbury Cinema in the King Edward Hall. Finally Oscar Deutsch who Entertained Our Nation opened a magnificent Odeon in Station Road, South Norwood in 1937. All but two of the 34 cinemas in the borough had gone by 1987.

It was Croydon's airport which provided most excitement locally during the 1920s and 1930s.

Many of the great firsts in civil aviation history were connected with Croydon. Famous aviators such as Charles Kingsford Smith, Alan Cobham, Jim Mollison, Amy Johnson and Charles Lindbergh started or completed their epic flights at Croydon and great crowds flocked to greet them or send them on their way. Joy rides were popular at 5/- and the roof of the Aerodrome Hotel provided a vantage point from which to watch aircraft take off and land.

The annual events of most significance were Empire Day, when schoolchildren took their Union Jacks to school, and Armistice Day. The two minutes silence was kept by virtually everybody. At eleven o'clock on the eleventh day of the eleventh month traffic would stop. Bus and tram drivers stood by their vehicles and a quiet descended on the land. But the possibility of another war had become apparent in the mid 1930s. As early as 1934 three lectures on gas in war were given in the town, and in 1935 a gas mask drill was held by the local British Red Cross Division. In the same year, following a Home Office circular, the town council set up an Air Raid Precautions Committee. Recruiting for fire fighting and for medical and decontamination units started, and Air Raid Wardens were appointed. Air Raid Report Centres were established in 1938. The issue of gas masks to the whole population began in September. By the end of the year over 5000 people in Croydon had been trained in civil defence.

1939 saw great activity in the provision of air raid shelters, with trenches dug in Blake's Meadow, on Duppas Hill, in Grange Wood, on Woodside Green and in several other recreation grounds. Other large shelters proposed by the town council were not approved by the Home Office in the belief that Croydon was not an area of maximum risk. Incredibly, it was not even proposed to evacuate the local schoolchildren until a council deputation to the Home Office brought about a change of mind.

On Sunday 3rd September 1939 Britain declared war on Germany. Perhaps it was just as well that Croydonians could not foresee the extent to which their town would be under attack, their lives disrupted and their loved ones killed during the coming six years.

2 Unveiling war memorial – 21st October 1921
The Lord Lieutenant of Surrey, Lord Ashcombe performed the ceremony and the memorial outside the town hall in Katharine Street was dedicated by the Bishop of Croydon, the Right Revd. H.H. Pereira. The guard of honour was formed by a detachment of the 4th Queen's Territorials. The Borough Cadet Corps, the Surrey Yeomanry, and ex-servicemen's organisations were present with a very large crowd including relatives of Croydonians killed in the war. Designed by Paul Montford (1863 – 1938) the memorial cost £5000 and was erected by Messrs Grace and Marsh.

3 View from Pollards Hill − 1921 *(above)*
The name probably derives from the trees which were farmed or pollarded to provide straight timber. This photograph was taken from the small recreation ground which was given to Croydon Corporation in 1913 when the surrounding estate was being developed. The view looking west across to Mitcham Common and beyond was still almost entirely rural.

4 Gravel Hill, Addington − 8th September 1934 *(right)*
The kiss gate on the south east side of Gravel Hill gave access to a footpath which crossed two fields diagonally to Selsdon Park Road. There is no trace of this part of the footpath today. The field entrance was a little below the flint and stone lodge to Heathfield which still stands. The road was widened to a dual-carriageway in the late 1930s.

5 Howden Road, South Norwood in the 1920s *(below)*
The unmade road with remnants of farmland on the right are reminders that much of north Croydon was still partly rural into the 1920s and 1930s. Norwood Lake can be seen on the other side of Auckland Road beyond the grounds of Norwood Club. The lake is artificial and was created as a reservoir for the Croydon Canal in 1809.

6 North End about 1926 (*above*)
Looking south from near the corner of
Drummond Road, the scene is still easily
recognisable sixty years later. The Caterham
bus is by the entrance to the Whitgift School
(now the Whitgift Centre). Burtons remains,
but the billiard hall then traditionally provided
above most of the company's shops has gone.

Allders' facade, complete with flagpoles, the
Whitgift Hospital, and the town hall clock
tower are virtually unchanged but the
Drummond Centre now occupies the right
hand side beyond the clock.

7 North End about 1922 (*below*)
Looking north from outside Allders just before
the store was rebuilt, the domed building on
the right is the Scala Cinema. This was
incorporated in the new store (see illustration
9 opposite)..The North End Hall, entered
through Kennards' frontage, left, was the
home of the North End Brotherhood and later
became the Civic Hall.

Around the Town

8 George Street about 1923 *(right)*
Looking towards East Croydon station from approximately halfway along the western end of George Street, the clock tower of John Thrift's warehouse was a prominent landmark beyond the Public Halls, and stood near Dingwall Road. Most of the business concerns have been replaced by others. The car facing the camera is a 1922 Lancia. George Street was named after the George Inn which stood at the corner of High Street opposite the Whitgift Hospital.

9 North End about 1936 *(below)*
Viewed from the bottom of George Street, a southbound 42 tram negotiates the single track through the bottle-neck between the Whitgift Hospital, founded by Archbishop John Whitgift in 1596, and the Crown Inn, now demolished.

By now, Allders store founded by Joshua Allder in 1862, had been rebuilt and incorporated the Scala cinema. This closed in 1953 and became Allders' china and glass department, later reconstructed.

The traffic lights were probably the first in the town.

10   High Street – 1935 *(left)*
This photograph appears to have been taken using a telephoto lens, from the upper side windows of Allders store, with the chimneys and roof of the Whitgift Hospital in the foreground. Crown Hill is on the right, still with its granite sett surface. The building occupied by Saxone on the corner was demolished, and the road widened shortly afterwards. The advertisement on the side, for the Croydon Empire is for the week commencing 2nd September. The programme included the film Carnival Night starring Jimmy Durante, and live appearances by Fred Sylvester and his Nephews, Wensley and Dale, and the Empire Band.

12   High Street – 31st March 1927 *(right)*
Looking north, the late 18th century facade on the right is Nalder and Collyers' brewery, with the Grand Theatre of 1896 beyond. The shops facing the theatre across the narrow street with its single track for the trams are part of Grand Parade. This extended from Meadow Stile (the entrance to which is between M. Banoff and G.H. Howard's shops) to Laud Street with Helling's Dairy on the corner. With the 1930 High Street widening, Grand Parade was demolished, and the tram track was doubled. Nalders ceased brewing in 1936 and the brewery site is now part of the Leon House complex which dominates this part of High Street. Grosvenor House is on the site of the Grand Theatre which closed in 1959.

11   High Street and Davis Theatre about 1930 *(below left)*
The Davis Theatre was the first outside the west end of London to be designed on American lines with a very large balcony, underneath which was a small mezzanine known as the Royal Circle and also containing the projection box. Designed by the prominent architect, Robert Cromie, and with 3678 seats, it was the largest picture theatre in England and the second largest in Europe at the time. The Davis opened with cine-variety consisting of two feature films, a stage production, and music provided by Charles Williams and the Davis Symphony Orchestra, and an organ interlude by Alex Taylor on the magnificent Compton. This cost 1s 0d, or 6d in the afternoon.

There was also a café restaurant surmounted by an illuminated dome and with a small area for dancing at one end.

Opened in 1928, the theatre was replaced by an office block in 1959, appropriately named Davis House.

At the time of this photograph the High Street was being widened. The building on the right was shortly afterwards demolished and the pavement in front of the theatre made narrower.

13   High Street – 31st March 1927 *(right)*
Looking south from almost exactly opposite the same spot as illustration number 12 above, an East Surrey bus on route 414 is on its way to West Croydon Station. The tram track was double again from this point. Beyond the Georgian houses is Masons Avenue and Crowleys' brewery with its chimney. It closed in 1929 and the buildings opposite including Crowleys' stables were demolished in 1930 for the street widening.

14 East Croydon Station about 1936 *(left)*
Originally opened in 1841, the station was rebuilt in 1894. The frontage did not change greatly until the station was rebuilt in a striking modern style in 1991/2.

15 Park Lane – 1936 *(centre left)*
The building on the corner of Park Street (left) was the town's main fire station and included living accommodation for more than a dozen firemen and officers. St George's House now occupies the site. Apart from those on the left of the bus all the other buildings have gone and the underpass is on the right.

16 Pump Pail about 1934 *(below)*
17 Union Street – January 1934
    (above right)
18 Numbers 11 to 14 Hill Street –
    January 1934 *(below right)*
The 1930 Housing Act eased the compulsory purchase and clearance of the older and more dilapidated parts of Croydon, many of which were in Old Town.

Pump Pail (16) ran north east from the junction of Duppas Hill Road and Old Town to Church Road. The partly demolished houses faced east on to a passageway. The photograph was taken from outside St Andrew's Hall.

Union Street (17) could only be reached by a narrow track from Old Town or a passageway from Church Road. The Parish Church tower can be seen in the distance. Salem Place and its council houses were built on the site but not on the same alignment. Hill Street and Hill Place (18) in the background ran up from Old Town towards Duppas Hill. Numbers 11 to 14 were at right angles to the road and demonstrate how 19th century housing was often squeezed on to tiny plots regardless of overcrowding, amenities and privacy. These houses appear to have a common passage separating them from their yards. The garments on the clothes line, not all of them pure white, are held aloft by a wooden prop cut presumably from a local tree. The grounds of Cromwell House flats and part of the Old Town dual carriageway now occupy the site.

12

The Northern Districts

19 Crystal Palace tram terminus – early 1920s *(above left)*

South Metropolitan Electric Tramways car number 40 is standing at the terminus in front of the south end of the nave of the Palace. These cars were fitted with special brakes for use on Anerley Hill which was one of the steepest anywhere to be used by trams. Trolleybuses replaced these trams on 15th February 1936. The enamel advertisement for Hudson's soap is a reminder of the housewife's standby for kitchen cleaning and scouring before the development of detergents.

20 Auckland Road, South Norwood about 1928 *(below left)*

The remnant of the Great North Wood in the background is now part of Beaulieu Heights and open to the public, but was then a private estate and the house which is just visible was in use as a school for girls. Building commenced in Auckland Road around 1873 and some of the older houses are in the background with newly built houses nearer the photographer. Apart from the horse drawn van and the corporation dustcart, traffic is absent. A dustman is carrying a bin and on the pavement are two dustman's baskets into which the bins were emptied. These in turn would be emptied into the dustcart which is a relatively small Shelvoke and Drewry vehicle.

21 Beulah Spa Hotel about 1936 *(above right)*

Following the discovery that a spring in oak woodland on the estate of J.B. Smith was rich in sulphate of magnesia, the land was developed as a spa, opening in 1831. On the other side of Leather Bottle Lane (now Spa Hill) the Beulah Spa Hydropathic Institution was built with 40 rooms and extensive stabling. Following closure of the spa in 1858 it became the Beulah Spa Hotel. The building was demolished in 1938 and replaced by the present public house, gardens, and car park.

22 Westow Hill about 1920 *(centre right)*

The buildings date from about 1860, following the erection of the Crystal Palace here in 1854. The street was dominated by the south tower of the Palace. Built to supply water for the great fountains and water displays in the palace grounds, there were two but they were not part of the original design. They survived the fire of 1936 only to be demolished early in the Second World War. The boundary between the ancient parishes and present boroughs of Croydon and Lambeth is in the centre of the road here, with Lambeth on the left and Croydon on the right.

23 London Road, Norbury about 1928 *(below right)*

Hermitage Bridge, where the road bends, marked the county borough boundary. Trams on the corporation's main route between Purley and Norbury terminated there and it was not until 1926 that the tracks were joined to those of the London County Council Tramways to allow through services to run.

The building in the right foreground is Norbury police station dated 1925, and like the shopping parade beyond has changed little.

The motor car is a 1927 registered Buick.

24 Whitehorse Lane about 1935 *(above)*
The triangular green on the corner of South Norwood Hill remains as a patch of rough grass, but was at this time neatly tended with stone edging, wooden bench seats, telephone box, water trough for thirsty horses, signpost with ornamental scrollwork and fire alarm (right). A Morris Minor van completes this view which was published as a postcard by Melbourne Davis whose shop (James — tobacconists and newsagents) can just be seen in the distance on the corner of Wrights Road. Well known in South Norwood, Melbourne Davis became a local councillor after the war.

25 South Norwood Clock Tower about 1924 *(below)*
The clock tower was erected by South Norwood residents in honour of William Ford Stanley to mark the occasion of his golden wedding in 1907. Stanley was a local benefactor who designed and built the Stanley Halls and Stanley Technical and Trade school adjacent to his house, Cumberlow Lodge.

Looking from Station Road to Oliver Grove, then with its ornamental pillars on either side, Holmesdale Road Baptist church is in the distance. The scene is still recognisable today.

26 Purley Way, Mitcham Road about 1930 *(above right)*
Looking to Thornton Road, with Canterbury Road on the right, the garage site was redeveloped in the mid 1980s and Sunningdale Court was built there. The large Lombank roundabout now occupies the road junction.

The splendid array of vehicles includes a 1926 registered Morris Cowley with dicky seat, between the motor cycles with their well protected riders, and an open Fiat alongside the garage.

27 Thornton Heath pond — early 1920s
(right)

The Wheatsheaf public house (left) was an early 19th century building and is little altered since this photograph, but in 1953 the pond was filled in and an ornamental garden created. The fountain was erected in 1897 to celebrate the Diamond Jubilee of Queen Victoria.

The lorry belonged to Worswicks of Croham Road and the open top buses to two of the numerous private bus operators of the period.

28 South Norwood High Street about 1920
(below)

Although the street is busy with pedestrians the sole vehicle in sight is a corporation tramcar. The boys are wearing straw boaters and probably attended a private school such as Raby Lodge. Cloth caps were more common in the 1920s and 1930s. The girls' hats appear to be the forerunners of the later straw panama hats.

**29 Woodville Road, Thornton Heath –
late 1920s** *(above)*

The shops on the left are those of the
Woodville Laundry receiving office, with
painted sign showing an operator and tailor's
press and then Charles Edward Searles, boot
repairer, beneath the repairs notice.
Scratchley's ironmongers and builders
merchants is on the opposite corner of
Norwich Road. The spire of the Primitive
Methodist church (now demolished) is in the
distance. Note the handcarts and the postman
wearing a shako, the forerunner of the modern
flat cap.

**30 Georgia Road, Thornton Heath about
1932** *(left)*

The Beulah Park estate which extended from
the present Norbury Hill to Northwood Road
was sold as building land in 1870. However it
became a brickfield and housing development
did not start until 1923. Most of the new roads
were named after American states which is
why the area is known locally as the
Americas. Georgia Road was built between
1926 and 1932.

32 Lower Addiscombe Road about 1935
(above)

Looking east from the corner of Cherry Orchard Road, Morland Road is to the left and the Leslie Arms is on the right just out of the picture. The policeman is on traffic control duty.

Belisha beacons for pedestrian crossings were introduced in 1934 by Mr Hore-Belisha, when Minister of Transport. Vinicombe's furniture stores and billiard table makers were established in 1872 and remained here until about 1936.

31 Thornton Heath railway station about 1928 *(below left)*

Opened in 1862, the station was rebuilt when the tracks were widened between Balham and Croydon in 1902/1903. Mr West's cab is a reminder that such vehicles plied from the station until the late 1930s. A familiar figure in a black coat and bowler hat, he resided in Brigstock Road and ran a garage as well as the cab business.

**33 Woodside War Memorial –
9th September 1922** *(right)*

The mayor of Croydon, Councillor Thomas Wood Roberts, unveiled this stone cross to the memory of the 335 men connected with Woodside who had fallen in the Great War.

The site had been occupied by a granite drinking fountain but this was moved to the junction of Howard and Birchanger Roads, on the green, where it still stands.

**34 Thornton Heath High Street –
May 1937** *(below)*

The clock tower end of the street seen during the Coronation celebrations. The building on the right with an abundance of flags is the Pavilion Cinema. Opened in 1912 as the Central Electric it later became the Pavilion Electric, although this name could still have been confused with the Electric Palace further down the street. Eventually in 1956 it was refurbished as the Pullman but closed in 1961. The building survives.

The Southern Districts

35 Upper Shirley Road – early 1920s *(left)*
Looking down Shirley Hills Road, with the Sandrock public house on the right. Shirley at this time was still a popular venue for day trippers and Sunday School treats.

The public house acquired its name from a rock on which a preacher used to stand to conduct services for workmen in the early years of the 19th century.

Shirley Hills Road was widened in the late 1930s and the cottages on the left demolished.

36 Windmill House, Shirley – early 1920s
(centre left)
Seen from Shirley windmill, the house was built in 1876 as The Firs. Later renamed Heath Court, it became Windmill House in 1912. The house stood empty for some years before it was demolished in 1954 so that the grounds could be added to those needed for the new John Ruskin school.

37 The White Hart, Wickham Road in the 1930s *(below)*
The White Hart public house was rebuilt on the site of an earlier beer house erected in 1820. Two parts of the same stream fed the pond which was filled in to provide a car park in the mid 1970s. The main stream forms the boundary between the parishes of Croydon and West Wickham (and also the county boundary between Surrey and Kent). The White Hart is just on the Kent side of the boundary.

38 Lodge Lane, New Addington – late 1930s *(right)*

Lodge Lane was formerly very narrow and until about 1930 it had a chalk surface and was lined with elms. The first houses in New Addington were built for sale by Henry Boot on land belonging to Addington Lodge Farm, and the First National Housing Trust then continued development of houses for renting. Building activity in the area ceased in 1939 and was then resumed by Croydon Corporation after the war.

39 Farley Road, Selsdon about 1928 *(centre right)*

In the early 1920s Richard Costain and Son Ltd. developed what was called Selsdon Garden Village, and Farley Road was one of the new roads.

The development was advertised as 'Croham Heights' with glowing phrases such as 'Clean morning air is a daily tonic at Croham Heights', 'Ample room for furniture', 'Kiddies grow up strong and healthy' and 'There is sunshine and pure air at Croham Heights'.

Ballards Plantation is in the background. Note the unmetalled road.

40 Waddon – New Railway Station about 1937 *(below)*

The Croydon and Epsom Railway opened in 1847. The original station at Waddon opened in 1863 and can be seen further along the road just opposite the Waddon Hotel.

The new (and present) station building is seen here almost completed, but with work still being carried out. Note the horse enjoying a good feed from its nosebag; the cart was apparently being used by the building contractors. One of the new trolleybuses can just be seen passing the Waddon Hotel on its way to Croydon.

42 Sanderstead Road – early 1920s
(below)
Purley Oaks Road is to the left, with Briton
Hill Road to the right by the East Surrey bus.
Still a rural area, cattle with foot and mouth
disease had to be destroyed in a field near
Purley Oaks station in 1924.

41 Sanderstead Hill – early 1920s
   (left)
Looking down Sanderstead Hill towards
Croydon, with Purley Downs Road to the left.
Sundown Avenue now commences on the site
of the signpost. Hill Brow Cottages dated
1895 are little changed today.
   The East Surrey Traction Company started
running buses on routes S3 (West Croydon to
Sevenoaks) and S4 (West Croydon to
Edenbridge) on 16th August 1921, giving
Sanderstead its first bus route.

43 Addington Road, Selsdon about 1928
   (right)
Looking towards Addington, the house with
the iron railings is the farmhouse of Selsdon
Farm, now the site of a Gateway supermarket.
The adjacent farm cottages dating from about
1809 were on the site of the present car park
of The Stag public house. The fine old horse
chestnut trees were felled and the roadway
was widened in the 1930s.

**44 Post Office, Sanderstead Village –
   early 1920s** *(centre right)*
The cottage was converted into a shop by
James Frosel in the early 1880s and was the
only shop in Sanderstead until Cranleigh
Parade was built opposite in the 1930s. It is
recognisable today, although much altered and
sadly without its charming cottage garden. At
the time of this photograph it was run by Mr
S. Leppard who also served as the Parish
Clerk.

**45 Brighton Road, South Croydon about
   1930** *(below)*
Looking towards Croydon on a sunny summer
morning from a point opposite, but just north
of, the Purley Arms. The northern entrance to
Churchill Road is by the parked car on the
left.
   The tram lines have gone but this part of
Brighton Road has otherwise changed
remarkably little.

46 Brighton Road, Purley about 1935
  (left)

Looking towards Purley from the corner of Old Lodge Lane with the Imperial Ice Rink, opened in 1931, on the left. This later became the Orchid Ballroom, once claimed to be the largest in Europe, then Tiffany's and in the 1980s Cinderella Rockerfella's. The Council offices (1929) and the fire station (1927) are just to the left out of the picture. Apart from the shopping parade, the development included the Regal Cinema (1934), with 1600 seats, which set out to appeal to Surrey 'Matinee Matrons' with a café restaurant where they could take tea and toast after the show.

Just beyond the Regal was the Uplands telephone exchange (1931). On the right hand side, the trees hid an elegant row of Victorian houses some of which have now gone to make way for a car park.

47 Hayes Lane, Kenley – late 1930s
  (centre left)

Looking from the bridge by Kenley station, Yately House is the large residence on the left. It was for many years in the inter-war period the residence of Dr Walter Smith. It was demolished in the 1960s and replaced by a block of flats – Yately Court.

The part of Riddlesdown seen behind the house is now almost completely covered with scrubby woodland.

48 Brighton Road, Coulsdon – late 1920s
  (below)

Originally known as Smitham Bottom, it was not until the early 20th century that the area became known as Coulsdon.

This scene has changed relatively little although a modern supermarket has replaced the building on the left near the railway bridge. Beyond Victoria Road, on the right, is an advertisement for one of the numerous local tea shops now replaced by fast food outlets.

49 St John's Church, Coulsdon − 1923
     (right)
The ancient tower of the church is seen behind
the lych gate, and signposts point the way
towards some of the many delightful walks in
the locality, soon to be lost under developing
estates. The road to the church which is now
Canons Hill, finished at the lych gate and also
served the flint cottages which, between the
wars, were a post office and tea rooms.

   The war memorial to the 41 fallen soldiers
from the parish who were killed in the Great
War was dedicated on 14th September 1919
and was later moved. The wire fence has been
replaced by a hedge bordering Grange Park
and the 1958 extension to the church has
changed its appearance.

**50 The Tudor Village, Old Coulsdon about
     1936** *(centre right)*
The newly developed estate is seen from the
junction of Placehouse Lane (foreground) with
Coulsdon Road, looking to Court Avenue.
The estate office is typical of the period. The
advertisement boards offer freehold property
at £595 or £750 and smallholdings − 'Visit
our Demonstration Poultry Farm and see for
yourself'.

51 Farthing Downs about 1930 *(below)*
An informal conversation by a now vanished
drinking fountain on a summer day, whilst a
boy attends to his bicycle. New houses are
visible in Marlpit Lane and shortly afterwards
the other fields in the background disappeared
under bricks and mortar. Evidence of
occupation in Celtic and Saxon times has been
discovered on Farthing Down − still a
popular venue.

53 Purley, The Exchange − early 1920s
(below)

The well known Purley Fountain occupied the triangular island in the centre but has since been relocated several times and is now outside the Public Library. The buildings have not changed greatly but the cross roads is now very busy and the environment is adversely affected by the heavy volume of traffic.

52 Purley Tram Terminus about 1936 (*left*)
Traffic signals already control the traffic and a smartly dressed woman crosses the road with confidence. The tram is a former Croydon Corporation car purchased for through running to the Embankment when the tracks were joined with those of the London County Council at Norbury. London Transport had taken over all local bus and tram services in 1933.

The lively shopping area has altered in recent years but the bank (now National Westminster) remains on the corner and the International Stores has been replaced by the Woolwich Building Society. The United Dairies was for many years previously Welford's Dairy and is now an estate agent's. Note the fine sign, with pointing hand – 'To London'.

54 Peaks Hill, Purley about 1930 (*above*)
In this view looking towards Plough Lane, two delivery vehicles can be seen outside houses which have remained little altered. The small white posts seen here have all disappeared but are still evident at the Woodcote Drive end of the road. Although fairly typical of the high quality development in this part of Purley between the wars, some houses in the road predate the First World War.

55 Purley Tram Terminus about 1923
   (*below*)
As there is no signpost pointing along Russell Hill Road towards London this view must predate the opening of Purley Way in 1924. All the buildings remain today but it would be unwise to stand in the road and chat as some people are doing here. For many Croydonians before the 1930s a visit to Purley by tram was an enjoyable trip to be followed by a country walk and then a visit to one of the local tea shops.

People, Transport, Industry, Leisure and Passing Events

56 Casting bells — Wednesday
    30th September 1936 *(far left)*
Six bells were cast for the parish church that
day at Gillett and Johnston's famous bell
foundry in Union Road. The largest, the
Whitgift bell, had been donated by the school.
Mr S.O. Andrew, the ex-headmaster who had
retired in 1927 cast a 6d coin into the mould
and the Rev J. Kinnear of the parish church
did likewise, continuing a bell casting
tradition. The foundry ceased operating in
1957.

57 W.H. (Peter) Mills — 1937 *(left)*
His family came to Badgers Hole, Shirley in
the 1830s and he was born there in 1870. He
later worked in Croydon before joining the
domestic staff at Coombe House. After his
marriage he lived at Broadcoombe Cottage
which stood opposite Bandy Mount (Coombe
Wood) in Coombe Lane.
    Always known as Peter, he developed a
great interest in the local area and joined the
Croydon Natural History and Scientific
Society. A well known and popular figure, he
sang in the choir at Addington church. On his
death in 1951 at the age of 81, his papers
were donated to Croydon Reference Library
— they are a mine of useful local information.

58 Oliver typewriter factory —
    11th February 1937 *left)*
The American owned company started
business in Croydon in the 1920s and
remained until 1954, their factory in
Gloucester Road then being used by Newmark
Watches.
    This photograph of the machine shop was
specially posed and shows operators working
at drills, lathes, horizontal and vertical mills
and at benches. A feature is the belt driven
machinery. Mr Hoy, the machine shop
foreman is at the end of the gangway, and
local historian Doris Hobbs, is the second
operative from the left with her back to the
camera. She assisted with the research for this
book, but sadly died a few weeks before its
publication.

59 James Smart — making brooms in
    Shirley — mid 1930s *(above right)*
Bennett's started business in sand and gravel
extraction, and broom making in 1777 on a
site opposite the present Shirley Inn. Later, in
1888, they moved to Sandpits Road where
sand and gravel had been worked during the
18th century. Broom making is thought to
have ceased during the Second World War.
Bennett's closed in the late 1980s.
    James Smart of Sussex worked for Bennett's
from the age of 30 until he died in 1936.

60 Coulsdon forge — 1st August 1925
    (right)
Coulsdon forge stood opposite Lacey Green in
Coulsdon Road on the corner of the present
Waddington Avenue. For generations a focal
point of Coulsdon life serving the numerous
horses in the neighbourhood, it was eventually
pulled down in 1935.
    This photograph is thought to show Tom
Rivers, the Coulsdon wheelwright, working in
the forge where the metal tyres were fixed on
the wheels.

61 Building workers – High Street – 1926 (left)

This photograph was taken early in 1926 at 27 to 31 High Street Croydon, next to Smith's Yard. The former Red Lion inn, a 16th century hostelry which had occupied the site and latterly was Staples Art Shop, had just been demolished. New shops and offices were being built for the Pearl Assurance company. This building in turn was demolished in the early 1960s for the St George's Walk development.

The men worked for the firm of E.H. Smith of Wellesley Road. The foreman bricklayer, Jack Fox, is on the extreme right and next to him is Roy Billington who was an apprentice bricklayer. A stalwart member of the Croydon Natural History and Scientific Society, he supplied this photograph.

62 Bute Road – early 1920s (left)

A motor charabanc 'carriage with benches' outing for staff of 'Wheelers Pies'. Thomas F. Wheeler, bakers, traded at 128 Mitcham Road from about 1916 to 1931. This photograph was taken in Bute Road opposite the premises. A gas holder at Croydon gas works can be seen in the background.

John Bennett's Coaches of London Road continued until the 1950s and were absorbed by other operators who in turn became part of the National Bus Company. The charabanc is a Dennis with solid tyres. This style of vehicle went out of fashion in the mid 1920s with the introduction of totally enclosed coaches.

63 Fay Compton at Kennards store (left)

Between the 1920s and early 1960s Kennards was Croydon's largest store. It was advertised as 'The Wonder Store of the South' and promoted many varied attractions especially for children. Visits by famous personalities, including stars of stage and screen were regular events. With pony rides, a zoo and a restaurant with the attraction of Ida Santarelli and her Ladies Orchestra, a visit to Kennards was an experience which could be enjoyed without actually doing any shopping.

Much of the store was rebuilt in the 1920s and the style is evident in this picture, complete with potted palms.

Miss Fay Compton's appearance was probably part of one of the store's birthday celebrations, held in the Spring of each year. Born in London in 1894 she made her first appearance at the age of 17. By 1920 she was playing Juliet in 'Romeo and Juliet' at Her Majesty's Theatre. She was extremely versatile including appearances in pantomime and revue. She returned to Croydon in 1961 to play Mrs Malaprop in 'The Rivals' at the short-lived Pembroke Theatre in Wellesley Road. The little girl who has obviously just presented a bouquet was probably the daughter of one of the directors in the background.

Kennards became Debenhams in the 1960s. The whole site was redeveloped in the mid 1980s and is now occupied by Debenhams and the Drummond Centre.

64 'Paper Jack' *(right)*

Perhaps one of the best-remembered Croydonians of the inter-war years, 'Paper Jack' has been the subject of numerous letters and articles in local papers ever since his death in a road accident in 1935, at the age of 59. Alfred Ellis Preece was apparently the youngest son of a prosperous Cheam businessman and was a qualified surveyor who began to show the strange side of his character soon after the First World War. He started living in his garden and later in open land or derelict buildings, and clothed himself entirely in newspaper and brown paper. He held regular Sunday schools for children in fields at Beddington or Waddon. 'Paper Jack' was much loved by local people and after his death a memorial fund was set up and the proceeds given to Croydon General Hospital to pay for a cot in the children's ward.

65 Ernie Grazier – May 1937 *(far right)*

Ernie Grazier sold newspapers outside the Greyhound Hotel and Grants for 35 years until 1958. As a lad he was a groom footman and at 18 married and came to Croydon where he drove a brougham for a resident in Park Hill. After military service and injury during the First World War he had various jobs but became unemployed and took up newspaper selling. A familiar figure who is still remembered by many Croydonians, he was always very patriotic and usually wore his campaign ribbons.

In this view he is standing outside the Greyhound with his stall decorated for the coronation of King George VI.

66 Electioneering – 1935 *(centre right)*

During the week ended 12th October 1935, Herbert Williams, Conservative MP for Croydon South, addressed meetings at Mitcham, Pump Pail, a spot near the Red Deer, and finally at Layton Crescent, near Violet Lane, seen here. His platform appears to be the back of a van. An announcement for the date of a general election was expected. This evening meeting appears orderly but it was different at Mitcham: the indoor meeting there ended with the MP descending from the platform to deal with a heckler who discreetly left. The general election was held on 14th November and Herbert Williams retained the seat. He continued as MP for Croydon South from 1932 until 1945, and represented Croydon East from 1950 until his death in 1954. He was knighted in 1939 and created a baronet in 1953.

67 Presentation of portrait to Alderman Trumble – Thursday 14th May 1936 *(right)*

Alderman James Trumble received his portrait from the mayor, Alderman Arthur Peters in the Croydon council chamber in the presence of Mrs Trumble and their two daughters. The presentation was in recognition of 44 years' service to the town. When first elected to the council in 1893 he was the youngest member and was later mayor for four years. He was influential in the purchase by the corporation of Grange Wood and Croham Hurst and in 1929 he became chairman of the newly formed Public Assistance Committee. He initiated the Sutherland Christmas Dinner Fund, was a founder of the Croydon Voluntary Association for the Blind, and was a trustee of the Crystal Palace amongst many other public appointments.

29

68 Canons Hill – 27th March 1933 *(above)*
This fine photograph is by F.H.B. (Frank) Ellis who lived nearby at Pound Cottage. Much loved by the people of Coulsdon, he was twice chairman of Coulsdon and Purley Urban District Council and made an extensive photographic record of the area. This view is from the Old Lodge Lane end of Canons Hill looking towards the church, and demonstrates the use of horse drawn carts in road building. Canon Henry Granville Dickson, rector of St John's church for 33 years from 1896 until 1929, had to walk the local field paths on his way to preach at various mission halls in the parish. The path that led to his church was named Canons Hill in his lifetime.

Steam wagon – early 1920s
(right)

Steam wagons were common during the 1920s and 1930s and indeed could still be seen in regular use after the Second World War but were replaced as heavier motor lorries became more reliable. This is a Garratt built at Leiston in Suffolk — note the solid tyres.

The Croydon Foundry Company commenced manufacturing in Waddon Marsh Lane in 1920. Castings from the three furnaces were widely used by industry, ranging from engineering, shipping and motor car work to small parts for sewing machines. In 1924 the Waddon Marsh Lane address shown here changed to 66 Purley Way. The company closed in 1971.

Buses and their crews – 31st March 1927 *(below left)*

It was very common in the 1920s and 1930s for motor buses to start and finish their journeys on the forecourt of a public house, just as the horse buses had done. These solid tyred open top buses are standing on the forecourt of the Swan and Sugar Loaf. From left to right are a London General Omnibus Company 'K' type, a Tilling Stevens TS7 petrol electric belonging to Thomas Tilling, another 'K' type and a Tilling Stevens TS3A petrol electric. The crews seem to be enjoying a few minutes' relaxation between journeys although one driver is investigating the engine of his vehicle rather closely, while the inspector checks his departure list.

Tram at Addiscombe – 31st March 1927 *(right)*

Croydon Corporation car number 65 seen about to depart from the terminus on the last day of operation of the route. The Addiscombe tram service was withdrawn due to the dangerous state of the track and because much of it was single track with passing loops, making for rather slow operation. The following day London General Omnibus Company route 178 replaced the trams, and then subsequently became part of route 12.

This tram was built by Brush in 1907 and had 22 seats inside with 32 outside. On the open upper deck of most trams and buses waterproof covers could be attached to the back of each seat so that passengers could partially protect themselves in wet weather.

Note that the driver is attired for bad weather with a leather apron, there being no protection from the elements. Windscreens were fitted on more modern trams in the late 1930s. Many of the drivers and conductors were well known by name to their passengers as they worked almost entirely in the Croydon area. There are two more trams in the terminal stub immediately in front of the railway bridge which still advertised Bingham Road Halt on the Woodside and South Croydon Railway although it had closed in January 1917 and was not to reopen until September 1935. It closed finally in 1983.

73 Electric train − 7th July 1928 (*left*)
Overhead electric motor car number 3260 was built in 1911 for the London Brighton and South Coast Railway in whose livery it is seen here despite having been taken over by the Southern Railway five years earlier. Note the bow collector for current collection.
Advertised as 'Elevated Electric', these trains had operated from Selhurst depot from 1912 but only via Crystal Palace to Victoria and to London Bridge. On 1st April 1925 the 'Elevated Electric' was extended from Balham through Selhurst to Coulsdon North and Sutton. However the Southern Railway decided to standardise on third rail electrification and the last overhead 'Elevated Electric' train ran on 22nd September 1929.

72 Waddon Marsh – 28th September 1929 (left)

Viewed from Purley Way bridge, ex-London Brighton and South Coast Railway push – pull coaches are being propelled towards Wimbledon by 0-6-0 D1 class locomotive number 637.

The West Croydon to Wimbledon line was opened in 1855 and electrified on 6th July 1930. Waddon Marsh Halt was opened then and the new signalbox made the section box and ground frame seen here redundant. The line was resignalled with colour lights in the 1980s. The small hut to the left is a toilet. The Croydon Gas Company's repair works is under construction (centre top). The siding crossing Waddon Marsh Way served Waddon Mills. Croydon 'B' power station was later built on the left.

75 The first electric train at Addiscombe – Sunday 28th February 1926 (above right)

The railway line to Addiscombe (originally known as Croydon – Addiscombe Road) was opened by the South Eastern Railway in 1864. It had been intended to introduce electric train services from Charing Cross and Cannon Street to Bromley North, Orpington, Beckenham Junction and Addiscombe in December 1925. However problems with the electricity supply caused postponement of the opening. Here the first train has arrived at Addiscombe.

76 Fire brigade display – August 1936 (centre right)

Croydon Corporation had its own fire brigade until the formation of the Greater London Council, when it became part of the London Fire Brigade. In the late 1930s there were fire stations at Park Lane (headquarters), Long Lane and Thornton Heath, and 91 street fire alarm points (as seen in illustration 24, page 14). This photograph shows a demonstration at Park Lane, apparently using some sort of asbestos suit. Note the splendid helmets.

74 Trolleybus in Tamworth Road about 1939 (below left)

Trolleybuses first saw public service in Croydon on route 654 on 8th December 1935 when they replaced the trams from West Croydon to Sutton. This trolleybus route was then extended to Crystal Palace, again replacing trams, on 9th February 1936. With the advantage over trams that they did not require track, they were manoeuvrable, quiet and fume free. The tram route from Croydon to Mitcham and Harlesden was converted to trolleybus operation on 12th September 1937, and the overhead wires can be seen leading right into Pitlake. The local trolleybus routes were withdrawn and replaced by buses in 1959 and 1960.

77 Royal visit – 27th June 1927 (right)

At 2 pm Archbishop Davidson opened the new outpatients, casualty and pathology block at Croydon General Hospital. At 3 pm King George V and Queen Mary arrived for a 1½ hour visit. They were greeted by 2000 guests, and the band of the Welsh Guards played appropriate music. The King and Queen spoke, as seen here, to many patients and staff. Queen Mary unveiled a stained glass window to commemorate the visit.

The walls of the ward seen here appear rather basic.

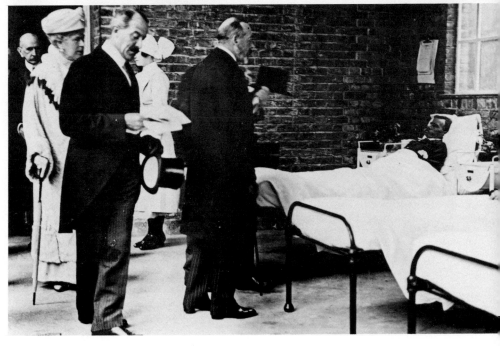

34

78 Women's Peace Pilgrimage – June 1926 *(left)*

The 'Law not War' peace pilgrimage of June 1926 was planned in January by 20 UK women's groups. Peacemakers from as far afield as Scotland and Wales assembled in Hyde Park on Saturday 19th June 1926. At each stopping place en route a meeting was held and the place name added to a board if a resolution was adopted urging the government to take the lead at the proposed Disarmament Conference at the League of Nations against the use of force in settling disputes.

The Peacemakers from the south coast and Sussex assembled at the Adult School hall in Park Lane on Thursday 17th June. The local meeting is seen here in Katharine Steet outside the town hall.

80 General Strike – May 1926 *(above right)*

The General Strike commenced at midnight on Monday 3rd May and was called off at midnight on Wednesday 12th May.

This photograph was published in the 'Croydon Times' on the following Saturday. The caption suggested that the strikers' idle moments had been temporarily relieved as the Croydon fire escape and firemen 'who have been loyally doing their duty' passed by. There is no explanation for the large crowd, perhaps because, as the comment about the firemen implies, the Croydon Times was unsympathetic to the strikers' cause. The scene is in Wellesley Road, adjacent to the old Ruskin House, looking south from near the corner of Poplar Walk. It is very difficult to visualise this tree lined, almost rural scene where now stand the wide carriageway and tall office blocks of the modern town centre.

79 Soup kitchen for the unemployed *(below left)*

In the mid 1930s an insensitively named Mental Defectives Institute ceased to occupy Robin House, 6 Morland Road. The premises were then taken over by the Croydon Occupational Centre. One of the first clubs of its kind in the south of England, it was staffed by voluntary workers and provided books, work benches, gymnasia and talks for the unemployed. It also had a somewhat basic canteen, seen here. The intention as expressed by the Honorary Secretary, Mr M.G. Philpott when he spoke to Croydon Rotarians in February 1936 was to give unemployed men an interest and a sense of purpose and so to restore their self respect. The collars and ties and clean shoes may be evidence of that philosophy.

81 Meat strike – February 1936 *(right)*

Croydon has long been important as a centre for the meat trade and in the mid 1930s seven companies of meat wholesalers (Borthwick, Swift, Weddell, British & Argentine, Tower, Armour and Morris) had stores in the Church Street and Frith Road area.

In early February 1936 there was a strike of Smithfield porters and at once Croydon became what the Croydon Advertiser described as the principal centre for meat distribution in the south of England. For several days, lorries, vans and steam wagons descended on the area and sides of beef and carcases of lamb were piled on the pavements.

This view is looking east up Church Street from a window of the Gun public house on the corner of Old Palace Road. Note the pendant lamps and the boot as a shop sign above Pearson's, the bootmakers.

82 Crystal Palace football players *(left)*
Players in training during August 1935 for the coming football season at Selhurst Park. Under their new manager Tom Bromilow, a former Liverpool player who had played for England eleven times, they were no doubt hoping for promotion to Division II. This did not happen until 1964 after 40 years at Selhurst Park.

The houses of Ross Road and the trees of Grange Wood crown the Norwood Hills in the background.

83 London Road, Norbury — 14th August 1931 *(centre left)*
Thundery weather conditions brought twelve hours of continuous rain in the town. Flooding was at its worst in Norbury where a lake of water between three and four feet deep covered London Road between the cinema and the public library. Three Corporation trams appear to be hesitating at the brink — with electrical equipment beneath the vehicles, considerable care had to be taken in such conditions.

84 Experiment with dustbin bags about 1930 *(below left)*
This photograph from the Croydon Public Libraries collection contains few details. It apparently shows a demonstration to officers and members of the council of the use of bags in dustbins. It was 1971 before such arrangements were introduced on a permanent basis in parts of the town.

85 Purley Way swimming pool about 1936 *(above right)*
Opened on 20th July 1935, the pool was 200 feet long and 70 feet wide. It cost just over £15,600 and could accommodate 1200 people. The charges in 1935 were 1s 0d for adults on Sundays, Thurdays and public holidays, and 6d on other days. In 1935 swim wear covered more of the body than it does today.

By 1973 major repairs were urgent: the pool closed in 1979.

86 Crystal Palace fire *(right)*
The Crystal Palace dominated Upper Norwood for 86 years. Originally erected in Hyde Park for the Great Exhibition of 1851, it had been re-erected on an enlarged basis at Sydenham Hill in 1854. On the evening of Monday 30th November 1936 a red glow was noticed and by 8.00 pm flames were leaping 300 feet into the air. Some 90 fire appliances and 380 firemen — nearly half the total strength in London — attended. The work of the fire brigades and 750 police was hampered by the vast crowds that came from miles around; the glow of the fire could be seen as far away as Brighton.

By about 8.30 pm the central transept had collapsed and there was no hope of containing the fire. It was the end of the country's foremost concert and exhibition centre and a much loved local landmark.

87 Jubilee of Incorporation – 9th June 1933 (above)
Celebration of the fiftieth anniversary of Croydon's incorporation as a borough included a visit by Prince George to the town hall, and to lay the foundation stone for an extension to Croydon General Hospital.

Here Katharine Street is decorated for the occasion and the original coat of arms of the County Borough with the motto 'Sanitate Crescamus' is conspicuous at the centre of the archway.

88 Opening of Savoy cinema, Broad Green – 9th March 1936 (below left)
The Savoy in London Road was the first of two cinemas to be opened by the Associated British Cinemas chain in Croydon. Designed by ABC house architect William Glen, it had a most imposing exterior but the interior was a little disappointing by Glen's standards.

Crowds flocked to the opening on 9th March 1936 and the Savoy was soon established as one of the town's most popular cinemas. The choice of site was obviously a good one as the cinema continued to flourish despite the advent of television. It was just about the first of the chain to be renamed ABC, and since 1972 has been a triple-screen cinema.

89 Coronation illuminations – May 1937 (right)
Here the town hall is illuminated for the coronation of King George VI. The arch appears to be the same as that used for the jubilee of incorporation in 1933 (see illustration 87).

The Croydon Advertiser reported that the main thoroughfares of Croydon were a study in red, white and blue. The corporation used 50,000 lamps in their displays and this represented only part of the illuminations which lasted for two weeks. Many of the features were borrowed from Southend on Sea. It was reported that two million people visited the illuminations and 33,000 cars were in or passed through the town on the last night. Katharine Street was so crowded that at one time it nearly had to be closed to pedestrians. It was also claimed that 60,000 people passed through Grange Wood in two hours to view the illuminations there.

90 Streets of Adventure Carnival about 1937 (right)
In 1927 Croydon District Traders inaugurated the 'Streets of Adventure' carnival, so named after a popular book by Sir Philip Gibbs. Held annually on a summer Wednesday afternoon (early closing day), it became a red letter day in the local calendar.

Here part of the mile long parade is seen moving from George Street on its way to Wandle Park. Up to the Second World War, when it was discontinued, over £25,000 was raised for Croydon General Hospital.

91 Aerial view of town centre – 1926
(previous pages 40 and 41)
If it were not for the Town Hall tower this
view looking north-north west from above the
Scarbrook Hill area would be unrecognisable.

Top left is East Croydon Station with the
railway running south, and a branch line
leading to Fairfield Yard and sidings with
Blakes' Meadow on the right, where now is
the car park and Fairfield Halls. Park Lane
runs across the picture, just above the centre.
On the right is Mint Walk, the buildings (now
gone) throwing a serrated shadow on the
roadway being the town's first council houses
built in the 1890s.

**93 Croydon Aerodrome entrance about
1921** *(below)*
Looking east from Plough Lane, this view
shows some of the early Royal Flying Corps
buildings. Note the advertisements for Instone
Airline Ltd. (1920-1924), Handley Page
Transport (1919-1924), and Daimler Airways
(1922-1924), which were incorporated into
Imperial Airways in 1924.

92 Croydon Aerodrome about 1921 *(above)*
The aerodrome was opened initially as
Beddington Aerodrome, Plough Lane, in
December 1915 as part of the Air Defence of
London. A separate airfield, Waddon, was
opened on the east side of Plough Lane in
conjunction with the National Aircraft factory.
On March 29th 1920 the combined site was
adopted as the Customs Air Port of London in
succession to Hounslow. The original Royal
Flying Corps buildings at Plough Lane were
used as a temporary measure and some can be
seen in the background, with the original
control tower. The Avro 548 (developed for
civilian use from the wartime AV 504) is one
of the many types of Avro biplanes which
gave pleasure flights for the general public.

94 Croydon Aerodrome about 1924
(above right)
Looking south east, this aerial view shows the
main hangars in the foreground. Plough Lane
runs between these and the main buildings and
airfield to the east. Aircraft had to cross
Plough Lane by means of the level crossing
(bottom left) which was later provided with
gates. The buildings of New Barn Farm on
which the airfield was sited are towards the
centre of the picture.

95 Aircraft passengers about 1922
(below right)
Passengers wait to board a Daimler Airways
de Havilland DH 34 G-EBCX. It was
advisable to wear warm clothing in the early
days of flying and these passengers appear
well protected. Note the wicker chair.

In the Air

96 Croydon Aerodrome – early 1930s
(above)

The aerodrome was reconstructed and formally opened in 1928, with new terminal buildings on the recently opened Croydon by-pass (Purley Way). The early buildings were demolished and Plough Lane closed and grassed over. In this view of the new airport the famous control tower and terminal buildings can be seen behind a Dutch Airline KLM Fokker FVIII PH-AEI and the Imperial Airways HP 42 G-AAXE 'Hengist', which are being prepared for departure. A 1930 Morris GPO van is also on the tarmac.

97 West Croydon Station area about 1925
(left)

The original station, with overall roof, opened in 1839 as a terminus, is near the centre of this view. After the opening of the line to Epsom in 1847 a second entrance was opened in the new Station Road. The station was largely rebuilt in 1932/33, with shops and entrance on the bridge and in Station Road. The supports for the overhead electric system are clearly visible (see also illustration 73).

98 Ashburton Park, Long Lane about 1933 *(above right)*

Lower Addiscombe Road is in the right foreground, continuing east as Long Lane, with Spring Lane crossing from left to right. Woodside Fire Station and its tower (right) is still under construction. Long Lane School (now Ashburton) was erected in 1929. In the foreground is Ashburton Park, bought as a public park in 1924. Almost everything in this picture was the responsibility of Croydon Corporation – roads, parks, fire station, schools and housing – at a time when local authority involvement was at its peak.

99 Croydon Electricity Works about 1931 *(right)*

Factory Lane is at the bottom right and then turns by the ironworks, beyond which Croydon power station (later known as Croydon 'A') occupies the right hand side as far as the concrete cooling tower. Opposite is the Corporation's Refuse Destructor and Disinfecting station of 1912. Two gasholders can be seen to the left. The Kingsley council estate under construction from the early 1920s still had no houses in Chapman, Thompson and Kingsley Roads.

Preparations for War

100 Home Defence Procession – Saturday 6th May 1939 *(left)*

The local National Service Committee organised a pageant of Home Defence to attract more volunteers to take part in training for the country's defence. Starting from Barclay Road, the procession was led by kilted pipers and drummers from the Brigade of Guards followed by detachments of the Coldstream and Grenadier Guards. Among the others taking part were nurses of the British Red Cross Society, Air Raid Wardens, Police, Auxiliary Fire Brigade, Auxiliary Air Force, Air Cadet Corps, St John Ambulance Brigade, Territorial and Civil Defence units, interspersed with bands.

From Barclay Road the procession went to Duppas Hill, where speeches were made, and then along Epsom Road and Waddon New Road to the top of Tamworth Road, where it is seen turning left into London Road. All main road traffic here was halted for a while and an address was given. The procession then continued to Broad Green, St James' Road (speeches), Whitehorse Road (speeches), Wellesley Road, Poplar Walk, and North End to Katharine Street. There the parade lined up to hear speeches by the Mayor of Croydon, Councillor Edward Stuart Baker, and the Mayoress.

101 Police War Reserve Recruits at Fairfield car park *(below left)*

Officers of Croydon Fire Brigade are seen here giving a lecture and demonstration on how to deal with incendiary bombs. George Street and St Matthew's Church are in the background.

102 Sandbagging War Memorial *(above right)*

A familiar scene at this time was of workmen constructing sandbag walls to protect important and vulnerable buildings. It was a sad reflection of the time that the war memorial had to be dealt with in this way merely 18 years after its ceremonial unveiling. (illustration 2, page 4).

103 Evacuation – Monday 4th September, 1939 *(right)*

In January 1939 under the government's Air Raid Precaution scheme, Croydon was declared a Neutral Zone which meant that no evacuation from or immigration to the town would be allowed in the event of war breaking out. However, following protests by the local council, the Ministry of Health designated Croydon an evacuation zone and plans were drawn up immediately.

At 5.30 pm on Saturday 2nd September instructions were received from London that transport and billets would be available within 36 hours. Around 18,000 people were evacuated comprising teachers, helpers, children under five years and their mothers, expectant mothers and the blind.

All school children were labelled, carried gas masks in their cardboard boxes and clutched their belongings. In the photograph a small boy is having his kit-bag adjusted by a helper. A World War had come again barely 21 years after the 'war to end all wars', and Croydon was to be in the front line to a much greater extent than in the First World War but that is another story.

Some notable local events between 1919 and 1939

1919   Croydon's first woman councillor elected (North ward).
           Peace Day celebrations.
1922   First woman included on jury at Croydon Quarter Sessions.
1924   Outbreak of foot and mouth disease amongst cattle at Purley Oaks.
           Purley Way completed.
1926   London County Council and Croydon Corporation Tramways linked at Norbury.
           Norwood Grove opened by the Prince of Wales.
1927   Captain Charles Lindbergh welcomed at Croydon Aerodrome by crowd estimated at 100,000 after record flight across Atlantic.
           King George V and Queen Mary visited Croydon General Hospital.
1928   New terminal building opened at Croydon Aerodrome.
           Addington parish included in the County Borough of Croydon.
1930   Croydon Board of Guardians ceased to exit.
           YWCA hostel opened in Dingwall Road.
           New offices opened for Coulsdon and Purley Urban District Council.
1931   New Whitgift School opened at Haling Park.
1932   Croydon vote on Sunday opening of cinemas − majority in favour.
1933   Croydon celebrated Jubilee of incorporation as a borough.
1935   Cattle market at Selsdon Road closed.
1936   Crystal Palace destroyed by fire.
1937   Typhoid epidemic in Croydon with 43 deaths.
1939   Outbreak of Second World War.

Sources and Selected Reading

The information in this publication is from many sources. Anyone wishing to study further the development of, and life in, the area between the wars should find the following of interest.

Broadbent, U. and Latham, R. (Ed)	*COULSDON, DOWNLAND VILLAGE,* The Bourne Society, 1976.
Croydon Advertiser	*CROYDON ADVERTISER* 1869-1969, Croydon Avertiser, 1969.
Gent, John B. (Ed)	*CROYDON, THE STORY OF A HUNDRED YEARS,* Croydon Natural History and Scientific Society. Fifth Edition 1979.
Gent, John B. (Ed)	*CROYDON OLD AND NEW,* Croydon Natural History and Scientific Society. Third Edition 1980.
Learmonth, Bob; Nash, Joanna and Cluett, Douglas (Ed)	*THE FIRST CROYDON AIRPORT,* 1915-1928, Sutton Libraries and Arts Services, 1977.
Cluett, Douglas; Nash, Joanna and Learmonth, Bob.	*CROYDON AIRPORT. THE GREAT DAYS,* 1928-1939, Sutton Libraries and Arts Services, 1980.
Cluett, Douglas (compiled by)	*THE FIRST, the FASTEST and the FAMOUS,* Sutton Libraries and Arts Services, 1985.
Baddeley, G.E.	*THE TRAMWAYS OF CROYDON* (Revised Edition), The Light Rail Transit Association, 1983.
Skinner, M.W.G.	*CROYDON'S RAILWAYS,* Kingfisher Railway Productions, 1985.
Whiteing, Eileen	*ANYONE FOR TENNIS,* Sutton Libraries and Arts Services, 1979.
Whiteing, Eileen	*SOME SUNNY DAY,* Sutton Libraries and Arts Services, 1983.

Local directories published by Ward until 1939 are invaluable for reference purposes, and local newspapers can be very useful, but it should be borne in mind that reports may sometimes be politically or otherwise biased, and possibly inaccurate.
The Croydon Natural History and Scientific Society has published Proceedings and Transactions since 1870 and some of these include historical papers.
The Bourne Society has published Local History Records annually since 1962 and these contain articles on the southern districts.

Acknowledgements

The ILLUSTRATIONS are from the following sources, and are reproduced by kind permission of:

Roy Billington	Number 61.
Croydon Advertiser	Numbers 9, 10, 14, 16, 34, 40, 57, 64, 65, 66, 74, 76, 79, 81, 82, 83, 88, 90, 100, 101, 102 and 103.
Croydon Public Libraries (The Croydon Collection or The Photographic Survey and Record of Surrey)	Numbers 1, 3, 4, 12, 13, 15, 17, 18, 58, 59, 68, 69, 71, 72, 73, 75, 77, 78, 80, 84, 87, 98 and 99.
John B. Gent, M.C.I.T.	Front cover and numbers 2, 6, 7, 8, 11, 19, 20, 22, 26, 27, 31, 32, 45, 47, 48, 51, 52, 53, 55, 85, 89, 92, 93, 95, 96, (all by C.H. Price).
	Numbers 5, 21, 23, 24, 25, 28, 29, 30, 33, 35, 36, 37, 38, 39, 41, 43, 44, 46, 49, 50, 54, 62, 65, 67, 70, 86, 94, 97, and back cover.
Handford Photography	Numbers 63 and 91.
Doris Hobbs	Number 56.
Ken Maggs, B.Sc.	Frontispiece.
Roger Packham	Number 42.

Many people have assisted in different ways with the production of this publication. Most of the research was by Ron Brooker, Ted Crawforth, Ron Cox, Doris Hobbs, Tony Moss, Roger Packham, Lucy Rogers, Guy Salt, Herbert Shaw, and Lilian Thornhill. Much of the information they obtained has regrettably had to be omitted due to shortage of space. Tim Harding identified many of the motor vehicles and helped greatly in dating some of the photographs. The staff of Croydon Public Libraries, in particular Stephen Roud, have been most helpful. Tom Mackrell of the Croydon Advertiser produced a number of photographs from the paper's files, while Tom Samson of Handford Photography, and Terry Cooper of Sheaf Publishing made some excellent copies of original photographs. Finally, Mike Hutchins and Tony Moss assisted with typing and general advice.

The Editor and the Council of the Croydon Natural History and Scientific Society gratefully acknowledge the help of all those mentioned above, and the work of the original photographers, the names of most of whom are not recorded, but without whose splendid efforts this publication would not have been possible.